I0624696

Where is the Church that Jesus Built?

Follow the Money

Another Shortcut by

Timothy Stevens

Follow the Money

Copyright © 2024

All Rights Reserved.

ISBN: 978-1-962849-68-5

Table of Contents

Introduction

One of Many Shortcuts to Find the Church Jesus Built.

Follow the Money

"If the Bible is true, it is of the utmost importance. If it is not true, it is of no importance, but it can never be moderately important." C.S. Lewis

This is a study on authority, with the main assumption being that the Bible is true. Of course, if the Bible is not true, the following questions are meaningless. If permission from God is required, for what purposes can it collect money? Does a church need the authority (permission) from the Bible in how or when it collects money? Can we improve on Jesus' instruction He gave to the church through His apostles in the first century? What is at stake if a church does go beyond God's instructions?

These are some of the questions that this study will investigate.

This is a very important study if authority is important. It offers one of the shortcuts in determining what churches belong to the Christ and follow the pattern of the first-century church and which churches are enemies of the cross (See Philippians 3:17-18) by not keeping the examples and patterns established by the Apostles.

This book may cause you to question the church you are involved with as patterns and examples of the first-century church unfold. If it does, it may be time to question your participation with that church.

There will be three different kinds of readers of this book. For some, this is going to be a very difficult study. For others, this study will be a real eye-opener, and still others will be bored to death because this study would be nothing more than a reminder of what they already know.

The reason this study is going to be difficult for some is because there are going to be certain practices of their church that this study identifies that they will want to defend, if for no other reason than it is their practice; therefore, it can't be wrong.

This is known as confirmation bias and is a problem that everybody has fallen victim to at one time or another. Once we state a certain position, right or wrong, logical, or not, our first inclination is to defend that position at all costs, regardless of the magnitude of facts or sound logic in opposition.

We would all like to think that we are above confirmation bias, but the reality is no one is immune. No one likes to be wrong, and it seems instinctive to rigorously defend ourselves even if we are wrong.

The way to combat confirmation bias is to welcome any challenge to what we believe and honestly evaluate it <u>in silence</u> until we have scrutinized all the things we need to take into consideration.

One problem we have is not being able to see everything we need to examine to come to proper conclusions, but there is an easy, quick fix… discuss a difficult issue with someone with an opposing belief. With this in mind, our verbiage in our objections and arguments should be done with great care so as not to put ourselves in a box, making it almost impossible to get out, and becoming a victim of what we are trying to avoid… confirmation bias.

Another consideration is unity or mainly the lack of it, and the concept that it is ok to disagree because there always seems to be some disagreement over something. We need to understand that it is NOT okay to disagree over Biblical doctrine, in as much as the Bible states that it can be understood (Ephesians 5:17). The only way we can come to a mutual understanding of the scriptures is to work at it, and keep working at it until we accomplish understanding and unity.

The amount of care is important in this study because mutual understanding doesn't necessarily guarantee that we are unified with God. If you haven't looked at Ephesians 5:17 yet, here it is, "*Therefore do not be foolish, but understand what the will of the Lord is.*" It's a simple verse with many layers of understated truth.

1. The audience is EVERY Christian at the church at Ephesus (Ephesians 1:1), applicable to everyone.

2. It's necessarily implied that the Lord's will can be understood by EVERYBODY. This assumes capability.

3. We are considered by God to be "unwise," if we don't understand His will.

4. We can "necessarily infer" that we have all of God's will necessary to understand what constitutes His will.

5. If two people are involved in a Bible discussion and they are in disagreement, they both can be wrong, but they both cannot be right.

6. Even if two parties come to an agreement, they still could be wrong.

If we have been told that:

1. The Bible cannot be understood.

2. We don't have to understand the Bible alike.

3. It doesn't matter what you believe as long as you believe in Jesus.

We have been told a lie.

Understanding the Lord's will is a daunting task, and we can spend a lifetime trying to understand it and the interpretation of the Bible that aligns with God's will, knowing full well that we will never be able to completely come to a full understanding. However, there is a verse (Hebrews 5:12), indicating there is a timeframe in God's mind of where we are supposed to be concerning the knowledge of His will.

The unsettling part of this equation is God could hold us accountable for information we don't know, with the time having passed when we should have known about whatever issue He is holding us accountable to know. Don't we wish we had been given a calendar when we signed up for salvation that gave us a clue of what we were supposed to know, and when we were supposed to know it?

When does accountability to God happen? I'm not the one to answer, as that is way above my paygrade, but I know it is different for everyone. Obviously, the 40-year Christian is going to be held more accountable for accumulated knowledge than a new Christian.

God does not divinely bestow knowledge for signing up for salvation. We are either going to <u>find</u> and obey the contractual conditions of salvation if we are able, or we are not. However, everything else is subject to growth. The problem is, when do we become accountable to God for what we are supposed to know? When do we become accountable to God in understanding what are the works of the church that comply with His will?

I wish I had an answer, but for most of us, I'm thinking that there is a point some time in our lifetime where we are expected to know what are the church's responsibilities and what are not. It would seem, for evangelists and elders (Bishops), that time would have passed when they took up their work. However, we need to remember that the Ephesian 5:17 audience, who was told to understand the Lord's will, was all the Christians in Ephesus, not just evangelists and elders.

If this study has found its way in front of you, it might be time to investigate what our churches are up to, and determine what activities of the church are within their scope of responsibilities as dictated by God, and not by us.

For now, we need to come to an agreement on the chain of command, the mission of the church, some important definitions, and some common sense "rules" for Covenant interpretation.

Chapter 1: The Agreement

We need to agree that:

1. All scripture is inspired by God (1 Timothy 3:16-17)

    a. The Apostles inspiration originated from God through Jesus (Hebrews 1:1) via the Holy Spirit. (John 16:13)

2. The primary mission of the church is to be the "pillar and support of the truth" (1 Timothy 3:15)

3. <u>Authority can only be derived from the "doctrine of Christ" (2 John 9).</u>

4. Authority can only be derived from direct Command, Example, or Necessary Inference.

5. God does not need to tell us what He doesn't want.

6. We adhere to established common sense rules of Bible interpretation, especially:

    a. Context

    b. Grammar

    c. Definitions

    d. Facts

    e. Harmonization

        i. If verses cannot be harmonized, and seemingly contradict each other, something is wrong with one of the interpretations.

7. We need to come to agree on what the first-century church spent treasury funds on, and when these funds were collected.

Unfortunately, if an agreement cannot be reached on these issues, there can never be a correct interpretation of the Bible, and this study, or any study of the Bible, becomes a total waste of time.

*Important Definitions:

Authority…

1. the power or right to give orders, make decisions, and enforce obedience.

2. a person or organization having power or control in a particular, typically political or administrative, sphere.

At 6 and a half feet tall, I can see the top of most refrigerators in most people's homes. Can you imagine me visiting friends and instructing the woman of the house that the top of her refrigerator needed cleaning? I did that one time as a joke to a friend of ours, and she told me get a cloth and some water and get busy. While this situation may be a little humorous, the ramifications are significant.

The point is that I didn't have any <u>authority or right</u> to instruct anyone on the condition of the top of their refrigerator and when it should be cleaned, any more than any of us have a <u>right</u> to instruct God on what would please Him, yet, that is what is done every day.

We don't tell God what will be acceptable to us, God tells us what is acceptable to Him, and we know that He will deal out retribution on those who do not know Him or obey Him (2 Thessalonians 1:8).

There's more.

Apparently, God doesn't care about what we think about doctrinal issues and doesn't seek or need our advice.

Isaiah 55:8 *"For my thoughts are not your thoughts, nor are your ways my ways," says the Lord.* **9** *"For as the heavens are higher than the earth, so are my ways higher than your ways, and my thoughts than your thoughts."*

Are we within the doctrine of Christ? …

2 John 1:9 *"Whoever transgresses and does not abide in the doctrine of Christ does not have God. He who abides in the doctrine of Christ has both the Father and the son."*

… Or, the traditions of man?

Matthew 15:8 *"THESE PEOPLE DRAW NEAR TO ME WITH THEIR MOUTH, AND HONOR ME WITH THEIR LIPS, BUT THEIR HEART IS FAR FROM ME."* **9** *"AND IN VAIN THEY WORSHIP ME, TEACHING AS DOCTRINES THE COMMANDMENTS OF MEN."*

Connecting the dots should be pretty easy for us. It would appear that we need to be within the "doctrine of Christ" having the Father and the Son, or be within the doctrines and commandments of men, not having either. This suggests that Christianity, if done incorrectly, could be a total waste of time if God is going to hold us accountable for what He expects us to know.

We can only be in the *"doctrine of Christ,"* or the *"traditions of men."* One of the doctrines will save us (James 1:21), and the other is useless and will condemn us.

Later, we will get into some classic Biblical examples of people who did and didn't understand the necessity of authority and were held accountable for not honoring God (Leviticus 10:3).

God's "authority" is absolute, and cannot be added to or subtracted from (Deuteronomy 4:2 - Proverbs 30:5-6 – Revelation 22:18-19)

Our authority is derived solely from the "*doctrine of Christ*" (2 John 9), which is only found in the New Testament. While the Old Testament is invaluable for getting to know God, history, and identifying the Messiah, it is not a source of doctrine under our covenant.

Jeremiah expressly states in chapter 31:31-32 that there would be a "*New Covenant*" that would not be anything like the old one. The New Covenant expressly states that any attempt to bring Old Testament doctrine into the new one results in being "severed from Christ," and the loss of grace (Galatians 5:1-6).

God has no use for our opinions, ideas, inputs, or our manufactured beliefs (Isaiah 55:8-9).

Church...

The church is the body of Christ (Ephesians 5:23 – Colossians 1:18, 24), a.k.a. "the kingdom of heaven" being the church that Jesus was going to build (Matthew 16:18-19), which was established through the Apostles, Jesus being the cornerstone (Ephesians 2:20). We cannot be saved outside of the "body of Christ" (Ephesians 5:23).

Faith...

Hebrews 11:1 *Now faith is the assurance of things hoped for, the conviction of things not seen.*

What is "hoped for," is something that occurs in the mind. The "conviction of things not seen," which is what is hoped for, results in an action. If there is no action, that means there is no conviction, which means there is no faith (James 2:20-24).

While faith is indeed works; works only indicate faith and neither faith nor works can "earn" salvation (Ephesians 2:8-9). If they did earn salvation, Jesus' sacrifice on the cross would have been unnecessary.

For a church or individual to be faithful, they have to do what they are told (2 Thessalonians 1:8).

Command...

For our purposes, a directive (order) from God that is not an option, requires obedience and cannot be added to, or subtracted from.

Example...

For our purposes, "a thing characteristic of its kind or illustrating a general rule." This is beyond assumption in the Bible, since we do not have to "assume" that an example that is followed is acceptable to God. God has demanded by "Command" that New Testament Examples are to be followed, or become "*enemies of the cross*" "*whose end is destruction*" (Philippians 3:16-19) if the examples are not followed. Like "command", following examples in the Bible are NOT OPTIONAL.

Necessary Inference...

Necessary inference means inference or deduced fact that is characterized as necessary. An inference is said to be necessary if another and a different inference cannot be reasonably drawn from the facts stated. It is a conclusion that is arrived by applying reason and logic to the collected data. Necessary inference means that such a conclusion was the only conclusion that could be reached.

A good example of this is in Acts 8:35. Philip is shown to have taught the Ethiopian Eunuch about Jesus. In the very next verse (36), the Ethiopian Eunuch asks, "look, there's water, what prevents me from being baptized?" Necessary inference demands the teaching about baptism is included in the teaching about Jesus.

In Acts 8:35, it is not indicated that Philip said anything about repentance or confessing Jesus with your mouth as Lord, which are also indicated as necessary steps to salvation in Luke 13:3,5, and Romans 10:9.

Because of necessary inference, we have to surmise that Philip also taught the Ethiopian Eunuch about repentance and confession in teaching about Jesus, even though they were not specifically stated like baptism was not specifically stated in Acts 8:35. Who would argue that baptism is any more important than repentance or confessing Jesus as Lord with your mouth? Not anyone I know.

Some might argue that baptism is not important at all for salvation; however, Acts 8:35-36 doesn't seem to support that very well. We'll cover that in the next book.

Chapter 2: Following the Money

From the Agreement #7

We need to come to agree on what the first-century church spent treasury funds on, and when these funds were collected.

Following the Money

By examining the facts surrounding the contribution in 1 Corinthians 16:1-2, and the goal of that contribution, we can see it as an <u>example</u> of an authorized expense. It was <u>commanded </u>to be collected at a certain time, and was an <u>expected</u>, <u>recurring</u> expense at the time it was collected. This will be important as other expenses unfold.

1 Corinthians 16:1-2 facts:

1. It was for Benevolence applicable to Christians in need in Jerusalem (Romans 15:25-26), and was sent to the church in Jerusalem.

2. The example makes Benevolence for Christians an authorized expense.

3. It was <u>expected</u>, <u>recurring</u> expense.

4. It was COMMANDED to be collected on the first day of the week, and is the ONLY "example" of collecting money we have for an expected, recurring expense.

Another example of collecting funds to help Christians in need is in Acts 4:32-35, and there are some important similarities and differences.

1. It was for Benevolence applicable to Christians in need.

2. It's an example of an authorized expense.

3. It was an <u>un</u>expected, <u>non</u>-recurring expense.

4. There were funds that were laid at the Apostles' feet, seemingly outside of the church treasury.

5. Sharing involved the whole church (32), meaning they were operating as a church.

6. There is nothing stating this was done on a particular day, and appears to be done over a number of days.

1 Corinthians 16:1-2 was for the needs of the Christians in Jerusalem who were affected by a famine, but there was time to collect the funds before they could be picked up and delivered, while Acts 4 is a case of Benevolence for Christians that required immediate attention. This <u>approved apostolic example for funds collected was used to help local Christians in immediate need where time, or lack of it, was a major factor.</u>

Another church expense involved assembling. We are commanded to assemble (Hebrews 10:25), which <u>necessarily</u> <u>infers</u> a place to assemble. A place to assemble comes with limited options like borrowing, buying, or renting, which could involve some expense that would involve a contribution to cover those associated expenses. But how would we determine when the contribution was to be collected for those assembly expenses?

Facts we need to consider about Assembling:

1. A place to Assemble is required (Necessary Inference).

2. It's an authorized expense that may require expenses

3. It's an <u>expected</u>, <u>recurring</u> expense.

4. We have an example and a command concerning when a collection can be taken up for an <u>authorized</u>, <u>expected</u>, <u>recurring</u> type of expense. If we are to honor the command and the example, and not become enemies of the cross (Philippians 3:17-18), we will collect it on the first day of the week (Sunday).

Another church expense involves supporting a minister.

Facts we need to consider about supporting a minister.

1. Right to be supported (1 Corinthians 9:9, 14).

2. It's an authorized expense (by Example).

3. It's an <u>expected</u>, <u>recurring</u> expense.

4. We have an example concerning when a collection can be taken up for an <u>authorized</u>, <u>expected</u>, <u>recurring</u> type of expense. If we are to honor the example, and not become enemies of the cross, we will collect it on the first day of the week.

These are the most obvious expenses that have direct apostolic approval. We also have to consider those things that take in non-direct approval by <u>necessary inference</u>, which would include tools like TV, radio, sound systems, classrooms, and projectors to evangelize. Cups for the Lord's Supper, songbooks (we are commanded to sing (Colossians 3:17 – Ephesians 5:19)), etc... Noah was told to use a specific wood to build the ark, but God didn't say anything about what tools he could use. We use this same principle today as we endeavor to stay within the "doctrine of Christ" (2 John 9).

If we establish authority by command, example, and necessary inference, then we have to make the following conclusions:

1. 1 Corinthians 16:1-2 authorizes the use of church funds to help Christians in need.

    a. Undisputable Fact…The only example or pattern we have for a church's benevolence in the Bible, <u>is for Christians in need</u>.

2. The 1 Corinthians 16:1-2 example authorizes a church to send funds to another church for benevolence. If there is no other example, command, or inference of any kind, a church does not have the authority to send funds to another church for any other reason.

3. 1 Corinthians 16:1-2 is the only example we have for an <u>authorized</u>, <u>expected</u>, <u>recurring</u> expense. This would be applicable to <u>any</u> <u>authorized</u>, <u>expected</u>, <u>recurring</u> expense in keeping with apostolic examples and patterns.

4. Any <u>authorized</u>, <u>expected</u>, <u>recurring</u> expenses can only be collected on the first day of the week **if** the example is honored. If the example, which is part of a pattern, is not honored, we become an enemy of the cross (Philippians 3:17-18).

5. Any locally <u>authorized benevolent</u>, <u>un</u>expected, or <u>non</u>-recurring expenses can be collected at any time outside of the church treasury. In the meantime, the church treasury could also be used in this situation and become involved because Christian benevolence is an authorized expense of the church.

6. Because there is no command or example for the benevolence of non-Christians, this type of benevolence is NOT an authorized expense of the church.

Notice, concerning #6, there is <u>no reference to "necessary inference."</u> It is because "necessary inference" would be the ONLY way to establish authority for non-Christian benevolence from the church, **if** authority could be established. This is how it is tried.

Chapter 3: Study Survey

Arguments for Church Authority Concerning Non-Christian Benevolence and Evangelism Practices

From here, we will address attempts to find authority for the practice of helping non-Christians with church funds under necessary inference. We will also address the Biblical support of ministers, which, surprisingly, is another major abuse in some churches.

We'll be specifically looking at these Issues:

1. Has God said anything about the church doing good for all mankind, including non-Christians out of the church treasury?

2. If the individual can do it, the church can do it, because the church is made up of individuals.

3. The epistles (letters) were written to churches, implying benevolent commands can be equally applied to the church or the individual.

    3.1 The importance of grammar and personal pronouns in Bible interpretation.

    3.2 We (the church) are required to do "good works" for all men (Galatians 6:10).

    3.3 2 Corinthians 9:13 Liberal sharing with "all men," inferring the contribution of 1 Corinthians 16:1-2 was for Christians and non-Christians alike.

4. The opportunity to evangelize allows the church funds to be used in helping non-Christians, giving the so-called evangelism

opportunity the power to set aside the <u>command</u> to follow apostolic examples.

    4.1 Exceptions to commands, examples, and necessary inference.

5. It's a good work.

6. It's an expedient.

7. It doesn't say the church can't give benevolence to non-Christians.

8. Jesus is our example in everything, and provided for the needs of those who were not His disciples.

9. Did Jesus stop feeding the disciples that stopped following Him?

10. Sponsoring churches:

    10.1 Benevolence

    10.2 Evangelism

       • Can a church send funds to another church regarding evangelism?

    10.3 Church Autonomy

11. The reasoning behind why God has not authorized, through command, example, or necessary inference, church funds being used to help non-Christians.

Chapter 4: God's Instructions for Benevolence

Issue #1:

Has God said anything about the church doing good for all mankind, including non-Christians, out of the church treasury?

Actually, God has a lot to say about this issue, and has directly stated the differences between what the church and individual responsibilities are concerning benevolence, which we will be going into with great detail. This brings us to one of the first things that I heard concerning church funds being used to help non-Christians.

Issue #2

If the individual can do it, the church can do it because the church is made up of individuals.

Of course, this is simply not true and can be proven by looking at the scriptures identifying different "types" of widows and their care. "Types" of widows? Normally, we don't think about "types" of widows. However, the Bible is very specific about what "types" of widows the church can be involved with concerning their care with benevolence, while these types are of no concern for an individual.

Consider James 1:27.

James 1:27 *"Pure and undefiled religion before God and the Father is this: to visit orphans and widows in their trouble, and to keep oneself unspotted from the world."*

This verse has many things that should be noticed:

1. "Oneself" needs to be concerned about the needs of others.

2. This is not talking about just a "visit" by the term "in their trouble." It's talking about taking care of their needs.

    2.1 There is nothing stated about the length of help, which could either be long or short term.

3. Contextually, James chapter 1 is filled with personal pronouns indicating individual responsibilities over a variety of issues and ends with a reflexive pronoun, "oneself," <u>addressing an individual, and not addressing the church</u>. (There will be more on this later).

4. It is important to notice that "oneself" is not restricted to any "type" of widow that can be helped.

    4.1 It doesn't matter if she is a long-term hospitable Christian or even if she is a Christian at all.

    4.2 It doesn't matter how old she is.

    4.3 It doesn't matter how many husbands she has had.

    4.4 It doesn't matter if she has a family that supports her or could support her.

    4.5 It doesn't matter if it is long or short-term support.

<u>Every one of these things matters to the church.</u>

Consider the widow of 1 Timothy 5:3-10:

These verses have several things that should be noticed:

1. The instructions are directly, and unequivocally applicable to the church (9).

2. The widow "indeed" is required to be a long-term hospitable Christian.

3. The widow "indeed" is required to be at least 60 years old.

4. She is required to be the "wife of one man."

5. There is no family to help her.

6. This is for long-term help. (Short-term help has different criteria).

What would be the criteria for the church to help this widow in the short-term?

1. She would have to be a Christian if the command to follow the examples and patterns of the Apostles are honored.

Clearly, there is a big difference in the latitude of benevolence the individual has over the restricted directions of the church concerning long-term benevolence for a widow.

Chapter 5: Differentiating Between the Individual and the Church

Issue # 3:

The epistles (letters) were written to churches, implying benevolent commands can be equally applied to the church or the individual.

Is there any chance that the instruction of James 1:27 or Galatians 6:10 could be applied to the church? This is how it was put to me.

"It is unwarranted, and indefensible to assume that Paul and James were writing to individuals."

-James was writing to the Churches (James 1:27)

-Paul was writing to the Churches of Galatia (Galatians 6:10)"

Continuing:

"Assume that these passages are directed to individual Christians. On what basis are we required to limit as to commands only to individual Christians, when James 1:1, 2:2, and Paul (Galatians 1:2) are writing to Churches?"

Contrary to what is expressed above, it is warranted and defensible to assume that Paul and James were writing to individuals on the basis of understanding that the church had its own limitations for who it could help, which were clearly spelled out, while the individual had no limitations or restrictions. **If James 1:27 is written to the churches; scriptures that limit the churches' authority to offer benevolence to certain "types" of Christians (widows) under certain conditions,**

make those limitations useless and contradictory, which brings to question the validity of the entire Bible. Also, even with a limited understanding of grammar, it is easy to determine when the scriptures identify that the inspired writers are addressing individual behavior and responsibilities within the letters they sent to the churches.

What is "unwarranted" and "indefensible" is the implication that even though James and Paul are writing to the churches, they are not addressing specific responsibility differences between the individual and the church. What does it mean if James 1:27 gives authority to the church to help non-Christian widows, and Paul stipulates that only certain "types" of widows can be assisted under certain conditions by the church? **It means something is wrong with one of the interpretations concerning benevolence, or the Bible is worthless.**

The widow of James 1:27 could easily fall under church involvement in her care **if** she fell under the biblical criteria of 1 Tim 5:3-10 for benevolence in regards to the church. However, no criteria for this same widow concerns the individual: none, nada, zero, zip, zilch.

James 1:1-27, Galatians 1:2 & 6:1-10, are good examples of how easy it is to spot individual responsibility using personal pronouns, even though the letters are addressed to the churches. However, these verses are not the only times this is done in the scriptures.

Consider the audience in 1 Corinthians 1:2, *"To the church of God which is at Corinth,"* then 2:14-15, *"but the natural man does not receive the things of the spirit of God, for they are foolishness to him; nor can he know them, because they are spiritually discerned. 15 but he who is spiritual judges all things, yet he himself is rightly judged by no one."*

Let's not forget 1 Corinthians 7, again, written "to the Church of God at Corinth," concerning marriage, which is an individual action, not a church action.

Even though Paul and James were writing to churches, grammar indicates when they were writing to individuals within the churches. If there is no way to judge when the inspired writers are addressing individuals, and not the church, God would certainly be the author of confusion.

First, God commands us to stay within approved examples or be enemies of the Cross. Then, He commands or allows the church to take care of non-Christians outside of the examples and COMMANDS He has given us? If this is true, we have God speaking out of both sides of His mouth, meaning the Bible is not true.

Facts are always facts. When it comes to benevolence, individuals do not have any restrictions on the "type" of widow they can help, or anyone (Galatians 6:10). However, the church has clear and specific criteria it has to address with either long or short-term benevolence before its involvement with the care of "any" widow, and does not have the authority to involve itself with benevolence outside of the church.

Issue # 3.1

This argument aims to undermine grammar, implying that grammar is not essential in Bible interpretation.

This is how it was put to me:

"Personal pronouns are a weak argument. The letters written to the churches in Revelation are filled with "personal pronouns" and are addressing the churches."

The churches mentioned in Revelation are often addressed with the personal pronoun "you," clearly speaking to the church. There are several grammar rules around personal pronouns, though they can get detailed and tricky, especially when diving into different categories like singular and plural forms. Yet, it's straightforward to understand that the use of "you" in Revelation is aimed at communicating with the churches.

However, in addressing James chapter 1, it is just as easy to see that personal pronouns are addressing individuals <u>and are wrapped up in James 1:27 with a word that we would consider a reflexive pronoun, is self-explanatory, and is within the context of the rest of the chapter.</u>

James 1:27 *"Pure and undefiled religion before God and the Father is this: to visit orphans and widows in their trouble, and to keep **oneself** unspotted from the world."* (NASB-NKJV)

Forget all the personal pronouns and the context of James chapter 1. *"Oneself"* in verse 27 tells the whole story.

Let's not forget, which is very important; God has stipulated what "type" of widow can be put on the church "list" for long-term care. This means:

- The church and individual responsibilities may overlap in some areas, such as supporting the truth. However, their duties are not always the same.

- Once God has specified a command, that command is the end of any discussion concerning a stipulation.

This is another attempt to include church benevolence to non-Christians by clouding individual and church responsibilities, ignoring context established by grammar, and going beyond what has been commanded:

Issue # 3.2

We (the church) are required to do "good works" for all men (Gal 6:10).

- Is Galatians 6:1-10 referring to the church or individual responsibilities? Again, grammar has to be considered. Start in verse one.
  - (1) *"Brethren"* - *"yourself"* – Church or individual?
  - (2) *"one another's"* - Church or individual?
  - (3) *"anyone"* - *"he"* - Church or individual?
  - (4) *"each one"* – *"he"* - *"himself"* - Church or individual?
  - (5) *"each one"* - Church or individual?

- º (6) "*him*" - Church or individual?

- º (7) "*a man*" – "*he*" - Church or individual?

- º (8) "*he*" - Church or individual?

- º (9) "*us*" – "*we*" - Church or individual?

- º (10) "*we*" – "*us*" - Church or individual?

  - If Galatians 6:10 refers to the individual, there is no conflict with the established authority concerning the benevolence of the church.

  - If Galatians 6:10 is referring to the church, apostolic-approved examples are useless, with Paul speaking out of both sides of his mouth. If "*all scripture is inspired by God*," we also have God speaking out of both sides of his mouth.

- º How can we know with absolute certainty if Galatians 6 is not addressing the church?

  - Aside from the flagrant use of personal pronouns? The term "all men," a generic term meaning everyone, would include the non-Christian widow who is excluded from benevolence by the church through a lack of apostolic example, necessary inference, and church commands concerning what "types" of widows the church can support in 1 Timothy 5. For the Bible to be true, Galatians 6:10 cannot be addressing the church.

- Painfully, "good works," even done in the name of Jesus, without authority, mean nothing to Jesus and will bring condemnation (see Matthew 7:21-23).

Chapter 6: 2 Corinthians 9:13

Issue # 3.3

2 Corinthians 9:13 Liberal sharing with "all men," inferring the contribution of 1 Corinthians 16:1-2 was for Christian and non-Christian alike.

This is a legitimate point and the ONLY point that gives credence to the idea that the church can be involved in any non-Christian benevolence.

2 Corinthians 9:12 *"For the administration of this service not only supplies the needs of the saints, but also is abounding through many thanksgivings to God, 13 while, through the proof of this ministry, they glorify God for the obedience of your confession to the gospel of Christ, and for your liberal sharing with them and all men."*

We now have a real, very serious dilemma.

Indeed, this verse does "infer" that the contribution taken for the saints in Jerusalem was for "Christian and non-Christian alike" and looks like a direct conflict to every point that has been brought up so far.

If it does, and we can't harmonize this verse with all the other points brought up so far, we are wasting our time because the Bible is simply not true.

There is only <u>one way</u> to harmonize this verse to make it compatible with the verses and principles we have tried to establish up to this point.

Notice the wording in Issue 3.3 above, referencing the "inference" that the benevolence "was for Christian and non-Christian alike."

When establishing authority, we are not looking for just an "inference," we are looking for a NECESSARY inference, an inference in which no other conclusion can be reached, which 2 Corinthians 9:12 doesn't deliver.

We need to establish some facts:

1. This is referencing the contribution of 1 Corinthians 16:1-2, which was directed to the church in Corinth and had already been directed to the churches in Galatia.

2. This is a narrative of what the Corinth church's contribution will accomplish in Jerusalem.

3. The "liberal sharing" benefited "not only the needs of the saints (Christians)" but everyone in Jerusalem.

4. **Any funds sent to a group for survival purposes in a locale will benefit everyone in that locale.**

    i. The grammar in verse 12 indicates the funds were for the saints first and foremost, while verse 13 indicates incidental benefit to everyone else.

5. Once the funds were put into the hands of the Christians in need, there would be no way to stop the benefit to others, even if they wanted to.

    i. THE "SHARING" BEYOND THE SCOPE OF THE CHURCH WOULD HAVE TO BE DONE BY INDIVIDUALS WITHOUT RESTRICTION BECAUSE THE FUNDS WERE SENT TO THE CHURCH WHICH WOULD THEN RESTRICT THE DISBURSEMENT **BY EXAMPLE** TO MEMBERS OF THE CHURCH.

Can we prove the contribution that the Churches in Macedonia and Achaia made went directly to the church in Jerusalem or directly to "all" men?

- Romans 15:25-26 is emphatic about the contribution indicated, which was "*for the poor among the saints who are in Jerusalem.*" There would be no way for the churches in Macedonia and Achaia to know who all the poor were in Jerusalem, Christian or not.

- It would have been logistically impossible for the churches of Macedonia and Achaia (Greece) to send the funds directly to "all" men, especially if "all" referred to "all" the poor in Jerusalem (Romans 15:25-26).

- There is no command in 2 Corinthians 9:12-13, or anywhere else, to use church funds to help the needs of non-Christians directly.

- There is no example or pattern to use church funds to help the needs of non-Christians directly.

- There is no necessary inference here to use church funds to help the needs of non Christians directly.

  - While 2 Corinthians 9:12-13 does necessarily infer that non-Christians would benefit from this contribution to the church in Jerusalem, 2 Corinthians 9:12-13 does not **necessarily** infer that the funds were coming from the churches identified or even from the Jerusalem church **directly** into the hands of non-Christians in Jerusalem.

  - If we harmonize 2 Corinthians 9:12-13 with Romans 15:25-26, we can necessarily infer (conclude) that the "gift" of 2 Corinthians 9:12-13 was directed to the "poor among the saints" in Jerusalem.

  - The Church in Jerusalem would be able to identify "the poor" among themselves and would be able to help them within the established pattern found in the Bible. In doing so, as stated above, there would be no way to stop the benefit to others living in Jerusalem.

Here is the Short Version:

The indicated contribution went directly to the Church in Jerusalem, which dispensed the funds to the "poor" Christians in need for their survival, who then dispensed the funds back into their economy, benefiting all of Jerusalem.

- This scenario harmonizes with the examples and patterns we are commanded to follow and harmonizes with the narrative of 2 Cor 9:12-13.

- Romans 15:25-26 identifies where the money was sent to and who it was for.

  ○ **Romans 15:25** *"But now I am going to Jerusalem to minister to the saints. 26 for it pleased those from Macedonia and Achaia to make a certain contribution for the poor among the saints who are in Jerusalem."*

Again, there was no way to stop the benefit to all of Jerusalem through the hands of the individual Christians who had received the benevolence.

Chapter 7: Evangelism Authorizes Non-Christians Benevolence?

Issue # 4

The opportunity to evangelize allows the church funds to be used in helping non-Christians, giving evangelism the opportunity power to set aside the command to follow apostolic examples.

This is how it was put to me.

"Churches would have authority to care for non-Christian physical needs based on their efforts to evangelize."

This idea is taken from Colossians 4:5.

"Walk in wisdom toward those who are outside, making the most of opportunity" (NASB), which is in context with evangelism, but is this directive aimed at the church or the individual?

If the context is a consideration, would it be the individual's speech that should be seasoned with salt (6), or the church's speech? Would Paul direct a church to "walk in wisdom," or would this be more applicable to the individual? Is it the church that is required to "answer each one," or is the individual? Finally, who are these commands addressed to in verse one?

The church?

No.

Because not all of the church members were "masters" of slaves, derived from verse 1, contextually, the audience of Colossians 4:5 would be a smaller group within the church. This means the command of Colossians 4:5 was not directed to the church. The "bookends" of verses between 1 and 6 cement who is being addressed.

Let's ignore context for just a moment and ask if there is a difference between "*making the most of an opportunity*" to evangelize, or creating an opportunity to evangelize? Churches can "create opportunity" to reach more people with evangelism by utilizing tools like TV, radio, mailings, and booths at public events. However, can a church utilize benevolence to "create an opportunity" to evangelize?

The problem is having the authority to "make the most of an opportunity" because an opportunity has to be lawful before we can make the "most" of it. Without a command or example of a church utilizing benevolence as an enticement for evangelism, the only other source for authority would be through "necessary inference."

The problem with Colossians 4:5 is that it is a stretch to infer, let alone "necessarily infer," that "making the most of opportunity" gives churches the authority to offer benevolence to non-Christians to attempt to evangelize. **And this is assuming that the application of Colossians 4:5 is directed to the church.**

The idea was pressed to me concerning Colossians 4:5 was that evangelism, being the "most important" and main focus of the church, takes priority over anything else and being more critical than benevolence, can set aside the command to follow the Apostles' examples and patterns concerning benevolence.

Are we sure that evangelism is more important than benevolence? In the hierarchy of all commands, where would we place benevolence? Position # 2: Love your neighbor as yourself? Maybe under love (1 Corinthians 13:13), above faith and hope? If benevolence is a sidebar of love, wouldn't it make benevolence more important than evangelism? Indeed, Jesus said, "I DESIRE MERCY AND NOT SACRIFICE." ... mercy above duty (law).

We offer benevolence out of Duty and Love. Why do we evangelize? Out of Duty and Love? Of course.

Maybe evangelism is not "more" important. However, the authority for either is the most important thing we must consider when we contemplate an action for either, both being equal in all respects in ascertaining authority.

Maybe there is more to consider.

What is the efficiency of offering benevolence to evangelize? I have observed from churches who have tried that approach that it is not what I would call very efficient at all, with few opportunities to evangelize and even less obedience to the gospel.

But we might ask if even one is converted to the gospel, wouldn't that have been worth all the money wasted on the others? Of course, it would. How could we put a price on converting someone to the gospel? Don't we need to spend as much as we can on evangelizing?

What's the problem?

When we convert someone to the gospel through benevolence, what gospel are we converting them to? Are we converting them to a gospel where the importance of authority is stressed, or are we converting them to a gospel where authority is like the "Pirate Code" in "Pirates of the Caribbean" … "more like guidelines?" Able to be adjusted by circumstance on a moment's notice.

It might be that Jesus, in His infinite wisdom, designed a church with the least amount of drama by not wanting people in it who have been taught that it is viable to act outside the "doctrine of Christ" were conjecture is the rule of the day. Or, the kind of the people who falsely convert for the material things they believe others will provide them.

There is much more on this in the next chapter.

Chapter 8: Exceptions to Commands

Issue # 4.1 - Exceptions to commands

Is it possible to negate one command with another?

We see that David and his men ate the showbread, which was not according to the law, setting the law aside, but fell under mercy as a necessity, which was also part of the law (Matthew 12:3-7).

A practical application for us would be our command to assemble and the possible sin if we don't, but who would not stop to help a stranded motorist or help a neighbor with an emergency, like their house is on fire? Could we set aside the command in the law of Christ to assemble (Hebrews 10:25-26)?

Could mercy set aside the command of following the Apostolic examples of only using church funds for the needs of the saints? Suppose there was an accident outside of a church building in inclement weather. Could not the accident victims be brought into the building for treatment, violating the "law" not allowing church benevolence for non-Christians?

Characteristically, biblical mercy that sets aside a "law" is associated with a dire limited need, with no other or minimal alternatives, <u>and is always an exception and **not a practice**. Simple logic indicates that when an exception becomes a practice, it is no longer an exception, and we know a practice cannot set aside a "law."</u>

This is a very important key. Helping non-Christians with funds derived from the church treasury for evangelism is a <u>ruse</u> and <u>subterfuge</u> and is not an <u>authorized practice</u>. A practice that is really trying to bribe people into a study making us enemies of the Cross, because we are outside the established pattern (Philippians 3:17-18), and outside the doctrine of Christ, which means we don't have God (2John 9).

If evangelism can supersede benevolence restrictions given to the church, the non-Christian widow of James 1:27 could also be supported by the church long-term under the guise of evangelism. Suppose we can set aside the commands, examples, and necessary inference under the guise of evangelism opportunity. In that case, we can also set aside the commands restricting the church from anything under the guise of evangelism opportunity because of precedence.

This reasoning has allowed churches to build gyms and baseball fields using the guise of evangelism opportunity. It would also enable giving church funds away at the grocery store because it came out of the evangelism budget under the guise of evangelism opportunity. Hasn't it been done? Think again. What other doors could open? Where would we stop?

Reductio ad absurdum – How about church-sponsored strip clubs to evangelize? Extreme? Once precedence has been established, as in this case, evangelism superseding another command, it can be carried out anywhere. Jesus consorted with sinners; why can't we? If this sounds insane, it's because it is insane.

What can we conclude:

1. Benevolence and evangelism should be carried out with the same motivations and with the same attention to authority.

2. While there could be rare authorized exceptions to the Law of Christ under mercy, church practices are not exceptions.

3. We have no command, example, or NECESSARY inference concerning the practice of enticing non-Christians with benevolence for an evangelist opportunity. This makes the practice outside of authority, outside of the doctrine of Christ, and sin.

4. The terms "ruse" and "subterfuge" should be enough for us to understand just how this practice is wrong.

Chapter 9: "Good Work" Authority

Issue # 5 - It's a good work.

Good works do not, under any circumstances, authorize anything. If there is no command, example, or necessary inference, we are outside of the doctrine of Christ, and we don't have the Father or the Son (2 John 9). It's not complicated.

Matthew 7:21: *"Not everyone who says to me, 'Lord, Lord,' shall enter the kingdom of heaven, but he who does the will of my Father in heaven. 22 many will say to me in that day, 'Lord, Lord, have we not prophesied in your name, cast out demons in your name, and done many wonders in your name?'"*

Look at all the things that were done in Jesus' name. Were any of these things "good things"? Did they need the authority from Jesus to do these things? Does it matter? It must matter!

Matthew 7:23 *"And then I will declare to them, 'I never knew you; depart from me, you who practice lawlessness!'"*

If a work is not authorized, it doesn't matter if it is "good." It's still not authorized and is referred to as "lawlessness" by Jesus.

Chapter 10: Expedient Authority

Issue # 6 - It's an expedient.

Benevolence for the non-Christian is an expedient.

An expedient to do what? Have the church cover an individual responsibility? For evangelism opportunity? The short version is that for something to be "expedient," it must be lawful. If it is not within the "*doctrine of Christ*", it is not lawful, as it doesn't fall within the "*law of Christ.*"

It might very well be expedient to entice an opportunity for evangelism with benevolence, but there are some unintended consequences. Luring someone in with food (benevolence) will often require keeping this up to keep them, hence the expression I heard once, "Bring them in with hamburgers, keep them with steaks." Often, when the benevolence dries up, so does their faith, which addresses their motivation.

The bigger unintended consequence of converting someone outside of an established pattern is their eventual understanding that following New Testament examples and patterns is not always necessary and depends more on convenience and the "success" of the "program." Once this is entrenched, Philippians 3:17-18 becomes nothing more than a mere suggestion, which is exactly what has happened in many churches.

Nothing could be further from the truth. We are commanded to follow the examples and patterns of the apostles or be enemies of the Cross (Philippians 3:17-18).

The bottom line is that using church funds to help non-Christians in need is not lawful because it cannot be found in the law of Christ. The only exception to this rule is mercy, but once "mercy" becomes a practice, it is no longer an exception. <u>While mercy can supersede a law (duty) as an exception, a practice cannot because a practice requires authority.</u>

Even the application of mercy requires authority.

Chapter 11: "It Doesn't Say You Can't"

Issue # 7:

It doesn't say the church can't give benevolence to non-Christians

Please excuse my bluntness. This statement would <u>NEVER</u> come out of the mouth of someone who understands how to establish biblical authority. This statement is usually centered around the inconsistency of agreeing to rules of establishing authority and then forgetting about what was agreed upon, or the agreement was just lip service capable of being dropped when it interferes with a held belief.

When God told Noah to build the ark out of gopher wood, did He tell Noah he could not use oak, pine, walnut, or any other type of wood? Of course not. When God told Noah to build the ark out of gopher wood, that was the end of the discussion on what wood could be used. God did not have to tell Noah not to use any other wood.

<u>If we understand authority</u>, when we are informed what church funds can be used for, that is the end of the discussion concerning church funds. God doesn't need to tell us what we can't do, and we know that if we only do what He has authorized, we have obeyed His will. If we practice anything other than what is stated in the Bible, it is referred to as disobedience.

> 1.1 When God told Nadab and Abihu where they were supposed to get their fire from, did God have to explain where they couldn't get fire? For some reason, they decided it didn't

matter where they got their fire from, but they found out it did matter and paid for it with their lives (Leviticus 10:1-2). In verse 3, God stated, *"By those who come near Me I will be treated as holy, and before all the people I will be honored."* We honor God by doing what we are told, aka "faith," and not going beyond our authority.

Are we allowed to add or subtract from God's word? Remember, God's "authority" is absolute and cannot be added to or subtracted from (Deuteronomy 4:2 - Proverbs 30:5-6 – Revelation 22:18-19)

We need to remember that once God tells us what He wants, that is the end of the discussion. He could care less about our opinions or about our input (Isaiah 55:8-9). Everyone I have ever discussed the Bible with has either agreed or taught me that the Bible cannot be added to, or subtracted from, and yet some will turn around and say, "The Bible doesn't say you can't." … It's maddening.

Simply put, anyone who would use "The Bible doesn't say we can't" does not know the Bible, God, or how to establish authority.

Chapter 12: Utilizing Jesus' Example

Issue # 8:

Jesus is our example in everything and provided for the needs of those who were not His disciples.

Here is how it was put to me.

"This doctrine nullifies the pure and holy life of Jesus Christ because He provided for the needs of those who were not His disciples. Why would it be ok for Jesus to provide for their needs and not His disciples assembled as His body? He is our example in everything."

The answer here is quite simple. This might be a good argument if Jesus' body was/is the "literal" church. However, the reality is that Jesus, like any of us, can offer benevolence to anyone.

As His disciples assembled as His body (His Church), Jesus being the savior of the body (Ephesians 5:23), we understand the church, His figurative body, has certain restrictions concerning benevolence. For the church to fund direct benevolence to non-Christians, these commanded restrictions from Jesus through His apostles would have to be ignored. When in the history of mankind, when anyone chose to ignore God, has it ever gone well for them?

This is an important fact:

The church, Jesus' figurative body, was not in existence when Jesus was providing for the needs of those who were not His disciples. Jesus established His guidelines for the church through His apostles, who were given the keys to the church after the Cross. Jesus, like anyone else, could help anyone He pleased.

Here is the cousin to this argument.

Issue # 9:

This is how it was put to me:

"Jesus fed thousands; when Jesus stopped feeding them, many stopped following Him, but did He stop feeding them?"

Should an individual stop caring for a widow who is not a Christian and stop if she refuses to believe? Do we refuse benevolence unless there is an opportunity to evangelize? This has nothing to do with the church and benevolence to non-Christians. However, it is an excellent example for us, as individuals, in not giving up on people.

Chapter 13: Sponsoring Churches

Issue # 10:

Sponsoring churches

The idea here is that it is acceptable for a church to "sponsor" whatever "good work" or any ongoing perceived "need" it deems would be pleasing to God and reach out to other churches to help fund the project.

The first hurdle is that no "sponsoring church" is mentioned, or inferred, let alone necessarily inferred, in the Bible with either benevolence or evangelism.

Issue #10.1 - Benevolence

A prime example of a "sponsoring church" regarding benevolence would be the Church of Christ in southeastern Michigan, who sponsors the Church of Christ Care Center and oversees the Church of Christ Assisted Living and the Church of Christ Senior Living. In order to fund this project, they require a monthly fee from the residents, which depends on the amount of care required, and funds from any other source for donations, <u>including other churches</u>.

Are there any problems with this recognized "good work?"

1. As we have already examined, the only example we have of the church being involved with any long-term care scenario is the "widow indeed" in 1 Timothy 5:3-10.

   a. Following the command concerning the examples and patterns of the apostles and not becoming an enemy of the

Cross excludes the long-term care of the church concerning senior men (Christian or not) or widows who are not Christians.

2. This is from the Church of Christ Care Center's website.

   a. "Of course, at Church of Christ Care Community, Assisted Living, and Senior Housing, <u>we accept and respect people regardless of religious belief</u> and welcome your personal religious leader to minister to you."

3. The Church's primary focus is being the "pillar and support of the truth," not the care of any and all senior citizens. Consider the fire extinguishers in a hospital. What are they for? What is the main focus of a hospital? Firefighting? If firefighting within the hospital becomes an issue, the extinguishers are used. Otherwise, the hospital continues with its main focus. If a fire breaks out down the street, we will not see any fire extinguishers or hospital staff leaving the hospital to put the fire out. We can apply this same principle to the church, as seen in the scripture. Benevolent care from church resources is incidental to its main focus and is handled only when it comes up <u>regarding Christians</u>.

4. A church that unwittingly sends funds to the Church of Christ Care Center for the unscriptural benevolent care of non-Christians participates in the same sin of the Church of Christ Care Center, both becoming enemies of the Cross (Philippians 3:17-18). Recognizing the mistake and repenting may fix becoming an enemy of the Cross, but intentionally sending funds should be inconceivable.

Suppose we are to follow the agreed rules of establishing authority with no command or <u>necessary</u> inference. In that case, we are obligated to follow the examples of how church funds were disseminated in the first century between churches. This statement should be the end of the discussion on the use of the church's funds for benevolence.

Issue # 10.2 - Evangelism

Can a church send funds to another church or other organization for evangelism?

Suppose we follow what has been agreed on in the beginning about establishing authority by command, example, and necessary inference. In that case, all we need to do is look for what was done in the first century concerning how evangelism was supported. What we find, like with benevolence, are examples of what was done and nothing indicating it being done in any other way. Meaning there is no authority from example for another way to support evangelism.

2 Corinthians 11:8 "*I robbed other churches, taking wages from them to minister to you. 9 and when I was present with you, and in need, I was a burden to no one, for what I lacked the brethren who came from Macedonia supplied. And in everything, I kept myself from being burdensome to you, and so I will keep myself.*"

Here, we find Paul receiving money from other churches to support his needs, <u>with the funds being sent directly to him and not through the Corinthian Church where he was working or through any other entity</u>. He could have also been receiving funds from the Corinthian Church, but he had elected not to have them fund him. **Is there any wisdom behind this example**?

All the churches in Macedonia were very aware of who Paul was and knew exactly what Paul taught. They did not have any oversight over what the Corinth church taught. However, they oversaw anyone who did any teaching they funded and could or would cut off the funds if they learned of any false teaching. Of course, the motive for doing such a thing would be based on not wanting to be a part of any false teaching, retaining the principle of being the "pillar and support of the truth."

If the Macedonian churches had sent the funds to the Corinth church, they could inevitably find themselves funding someone they did not know and false doctrine(s), not fulfilling their responsibility of being the "pillar and support of the truth." While not absolutely foolproof, the pattern for funding evangelism mitigates the chances of a church inadvertently becoming involved with the teaching of false doctrines.

The situation would be the same if any of the churches had become a "sponsoring church" and collected the funds from the other churches in Macedonia for Paul, essentially taking over the oversight of the funds from the other churches without authority. This process not only presents all the problems above but also adds the possibility of Paul not receiving all the funds designated to him, either from fiduciary irresponsibility, administrative expenses, or even outright theft. Staying within God's authority completely eliminates, except for outright theft, these potential problems.

The bottom line is that the only reason a church can send funds to another church is for benevolence for Christians in need. The support of ministers from another congregation has to go directly into the hands of the minister from the supporting church.

Similar to the example of Paul and his companions, a common carrier could deliver this. They acted as the common carrier for other churches, aiding the Jerusalem Christians. This is the only way it can be done if we want to avoid being an enemy of the Cross.

At the time of the writing, a church in Northern Michigan accepts funds from almost any source, including churches, to fund their TV evangelist program that actually comes from a church in the south. Is there a pattern that would justify this activity? First, would TV evangelism be authorized?

We know that churches have a responsibility to evangelize (2 Timothy 2:2). Maybe Noah was specifically told what wood he had to use, but remember, he was not told anything about what kind of tools he could use. We are under the same principle with evangelism and have the authority to use whatever tools are scripturally available to help us live up to the STATED responsibility.

In **1 Corinthians 16:1-2** we have the responsibility to "*lay by in store as we have prospered*" "*on the first day of the week,*" but the "how" is left up to us. Using these biblical principles, we can infer that we can use TV to evangelize in fulfilling the general command to be the "pillar and support of the truth."

So, the problem is not using TV to evangelize; the problem arises from the funding of evangelism. As already stated, there is no command, example, or necessary inference for one church to send funds to another church for evangelism. However, as already stated, we have an example of churches sending funds directly to an evangelist for evangelism.

What is hard to understand is why not scripturally fund the TV program by having the churches willing to help, get to know the evangelist, and send the funds to the evangelist. This would mean knowing him, his beliefs, and what he teaches, and would follow the command to stay within the patterns and examples in the Law of Christ.

What a great teaching opportunity it would be to establish the importance of command, example, and necessary inference, but instead, they are teaching that the rules for establishing authority are not essential and not needed when it comes to obeying God and can be set aside for what is advertised as an important, "good work." Tell Nadab and Abihu (Leviticus 10:1-2) that God should not have punished them for their important "good work." Better yet, maybe we should set God straight on who has the final authority to authorize important "good works." You, first!

Issue # 10.3 - Church Autonomy

Church autonomy is based on Acts 20:28 and 1 Peter 5:2. In contrast to what is done today, bishops (elders, overseers) only had the authority to rule over the "flock among themselves," meaning they did not have any rule or authority over any other congregation (flock). It is a brilliant concept to protect all the churches from falling into a false doctrine at once, which is made possible by a central church headquarters. The church that Jesus designed and built has no central governing authority like some denominations, making it virtually impossible for a false doctrine to infiltrate all His local congregations.

Consider that a false teacher would have to go to every church designed by Jesus and would have to get their doctrine past elders (Bishops) who are *"apt to teach,"* one or more ministers, and a congregation who has been instructed to *"understand what the will of God is"* (Ephesians 5:17).

While it is possible to get a false teaching into one church designed by Jesus, already having been done, it is not probable. What odds would you place on all the churches designed by Jesus succumbing to a false doctrine? Personally, I wouldn't give you any odds.

Church autonomy, as established in the Bible, naturally limits and sets the boundaries of oversight and accountability. If a church is considered to be "autonomous" then:

1. Concerning benevolence, the sending church has complete oversight of the amount of the funds delivered and the delivery of the funds until the funds have reached the church in need. Autonomy is compromised if there is a "sponsoring church" or other like entity in the middle.

2. Once a church sends benevolent funds to another church, the receiving church has sole discretion, oversight, and accountability regarding how those funds are used.

3. Church autonomy establishes that there is no authority or accountability for teaching the truth in another local congregation. (Bishops only have oversight of the flock among themselves)

4. Biblical examples and patterns do not allow funds to be sent from one church to another concerning evangelism, and are required to send the funds directly into the hands of the evangelist they are supporting. Sending funds to another church for evangelism could very well come with instruction on what will be taught,

compromising the "autonomy" of the church receiving the funds.

5. A church supporting an evangelist at another location does not have oversight as to what subjects are being taught in another church but does have oversight of the evangelist and what he teaches through their support. By it being done this way, the "autonomy" of the church where the evangelist works is not compromised.

We see from the scriptures no middle organizations were taking on the responsibility (oversight) of seeing that the appropriated benevolent funds were delivered to the right church. Once another entity, like a "sponsoring church," is put in the equation, the opportunity for error, outright theft, or "administration expenses" becomes an amplified possibility. While direct delivery of funds is not entirely foolproof, it does mitigate some of the problems. In the case of "administrative expenses," that problem is completely eliminated.

The church that is sending funds to another church for benevolence has the sole discretion of the amount it is going to send, meaning the receiving church has no authority to direct how much is being sent to them. Once the funds are received by the church in need, the oversight of those funds by the sending church is over.

Because the church that sends the funds has no authority or oversight over another church, the receiving church can use the funds at its discretion. Because there is no oversight as to how the funds are used by the sending church, having been sent in good faith, if the funds are used in an unscriptural manner, only the receiving church would be accountable for its action.

Oversight boundaries directed by God are paramount, not only for obedience, but are put in place for reasons that become obvious. Changing those boundaries vastly amplifies the probability of theft and the misappropriation of funds, and worse, we find ourselves enemies of the Cross.

Chapter 14: What is Behind the Instructions

Issue # 11:

Why is there no command, example, or necessary inference for church funds to be used to help non-Christians?

Could we apply any logic to God's instruction concerning church benevolence?

We all know some people feign being religious, preying on the good-natured intentions of those who take their religion seriously. This has resulted in many of us being scammed, often knowingly or at least suspiciously, at one time or another. However, suppose church treasury funds cannot be used for helping non-Christians. In that case, the church can **NEVER** be scammed and money wasted by a non-Christian trying to take advantage of a church.

Another consideration is the care an individual would take or should take in helping someone else with their own money, especially someone they don't know. One way or another, if the church treasury is used to support a non-Christian, and the benevolence is a scam, it involves the entire church in the fraud, which is not really the big problem. The big problem is the disobedience involving the whole church.

Rarely is anything foolproof, but the facts are clear; if there are no church funds available for non-Christian benevolence, there is no way a church can be scammed using benevolence as the vehicle for the scam by a non-Christian.

Chapter 15: Parting Thoughts

Is God being cold-hearted toward anyone who is not a Christian by not authorizing church funds to be used for their care? There are a few things we should consider:

1. Do we have a right to judge God? (See Isaiah 55:8-9)

2. Do we trust that God knows what He is doing?

3. Has God given any instructions concerning benevolence toward non-Christians? Yes, He has.

4. Does it "feel" right to bribe someone with benevolence to become a Christian?

Before I became a "Christian" coming out of the Catholic Church, I had no idea there were 2 Levite priests named Nadab and Abihu (Leviticus 10:1-2) and their importance in understanding authority. We are reminded that Nadab and Abihu were told where their fire for worship was to come from. However, they decided that fire from one place was as good as fire from any place, so they brought "*strange*" fire to their worship. They paid with their lives for their arrogance in setting aside a command from God.

Maybe our covenants have changed since Nadab and Abihu, but our God has not…He still expects to be obeyed (2 Thessalonians 1:8), and there could come a time when we will answer for the lack of knowledge God expects us to know (Hebrews 5:12). God held Nadab and Abihu to a higher standard because of their standing as Levite priests, and God will hold us accountable to a standard that could, and would be different for everybody. Certainly, the new convert is not going to be held to the same standard of knowledge as someone who has been a "Christian" for 40 years (Hebrews 5:12) or is a teacher (James 3:1).

Because authority is so important, we need to ask ourselves some serious questions:

1. Does the church I attend know how to establish authority?

    a. If church funds are being used for helping non-Christians, that church does NOT know how to establish authority.

    b. If the church funds are collected for any authorized, expected, recurring expense other than the first day of the week, that church does not understand how to establish authority.

    c. If funds are raised from bake sales, raffles, or other "fundraisers," that church does not know how to establish authority.

2. If I were to follow the money in the first-century church, would I find the same money trail in the church I attend?

    a. Would it be collected on the first day of the week as the first-century church did? Or, will your church collect money anytime it opens the doors, showing their distrust in God to know what He is doing?

    b. Would it be spent the same way as it was done in the first-century church?

3. Could I be in a position of accountability for these issues?

    a. Consider the accountability of attendance in Hebrews 10:24-27. Once the new Christian comes to "*a knowledge of the truth*" about assembling and decides attendance is not important or necessary, what is the stated consequence of that decision (see 26-27). Having read this book and considered the indicated scriptures pertaining to the issues in this book, where do you place your accountability?

4. Are there any churches in the area that mirror the first-century church? If there is one, and you have properly connected the dots, you will be there this first day of the week (Sunday). There might be one right around the corner from you.

The path to becoming an enemy of the Cross is an easy path to get on and a hard path to get off. The path to pleasing God is a narrow path, and few there are that find it (Matthew 7:14).

About the Author

A former insurance agent, Tim has embraced the Christian faith for 43 years. He lives with his beloved wife of 55 years in a quaint neighborhood near Flint, MI.

One of the pathways that led him to discover the First Century Church was by tracing financial trails. While it is an important major shortcut, Tim has seven other insightful shortcuts in a book coming soon that can be utilized on a journey in searching for the church Jesus designed and is in existence in our time.

www.ingramcontent.com/pod-product-compliance
Lightning Source LLC
Chambersburg PA
CBHW051648120626
46551CB00015B/2265